AF521720

ground

rainbow

hour

seasons

hurricane

second

noon

sun

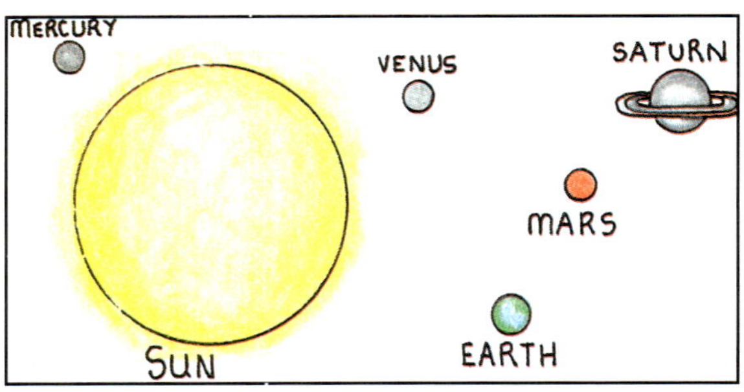

planet

temperature

rain

thaw

Earth Words

The Earth is the planet on which we live. It is the fifth largest planet in our solar system and the third planet in order of distance from the sun.

horse

fence

fields

forest

lake

lane

leaves

mountains

mud

nature

roots

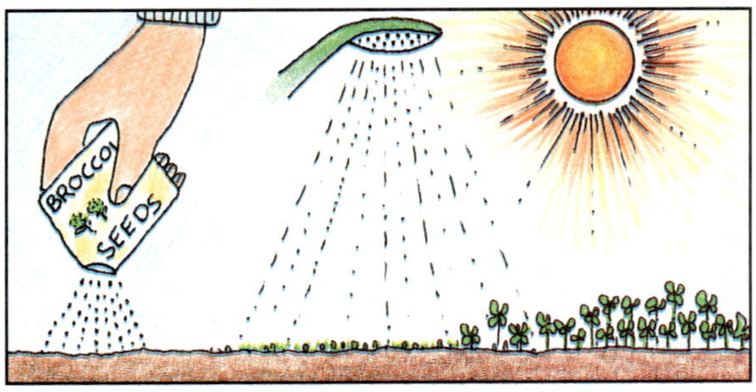

seeds

stream

Country Words

The land outside cities and towns is called the country or countryside. Farmland is part of the countryside where crops are grown and animals graze.

Easter

paddling

canoeing

fancy dress

paper hats

fireworks

pony-
trekking

vacation

sight
seeing

label

suitcases

skiing

camping

splashing

Vacation Words

A holiday is a day on which people do not work or go to school. Families sometimes spend vacations at the seaside, or visit other countries.

bridge

truck

bus

tunnel

carrying

van

taxi

walking

track

wheels

train

yachts

Moving Words

Moving words are about changing the place or direction of something; people move by walking or cycling or using other forms of transport.

camels

pigs

canary

rabbits

cats

reindeer

peacocks

reptiles

penguins

rhinoceros

pets

seals

Animal Words

Animals are living creatures made up of many cells, which take in food and move about. Unlike plants, animals do not have to stay in one place, and they cannot make their own food.

air stewardess

diver

artist

electrician

baker

factory

cook

store

cowboy

street

cranes

sweeper

Working Words

Work is the use of a person's skill or energy to do something, perhaps to earn money as a job or occupation, or to perform a task that needs to be done.

atlas

bell

black

chalk

class

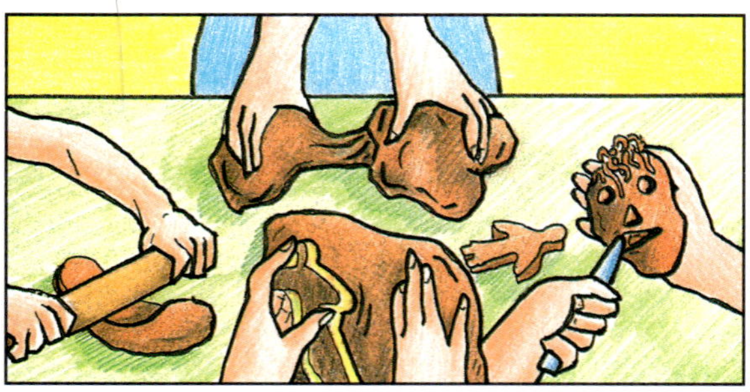

clay

copying

desk

dividing

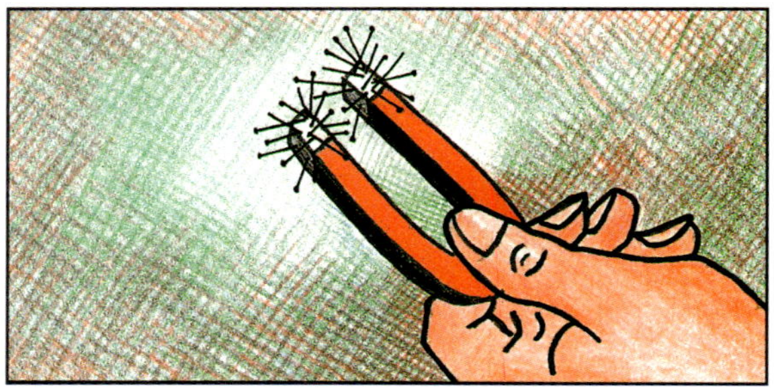

magnet

map

measures

Learning Words

Learning is knowledge gained through study or practice, at school or college where teachers help us to learn, or at home where our parents teach us and help us to grow up.

hopping

magic show

juggling

singing

jumping

skating

piano

skipping

picnic

sliding

playground

story telling

Playing Words

Playing is an activity which is done for fun and pleasure – we play games perhaps ourselves or with friends, and we play musical instruments.

meat

sausages

milk

soup

mushrooms

sugar

potatoes

toast

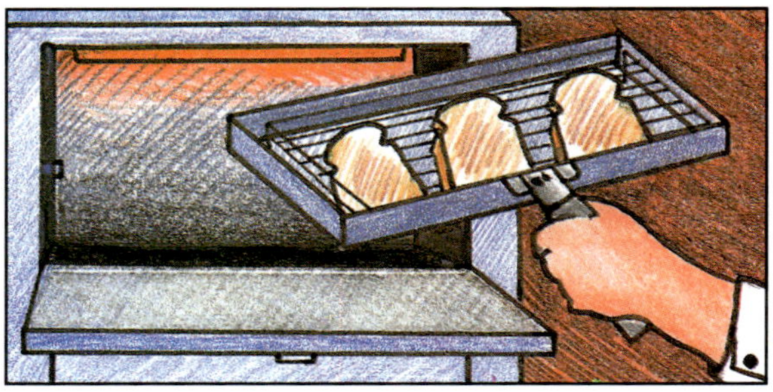

poultry

vegetables

puddings

water

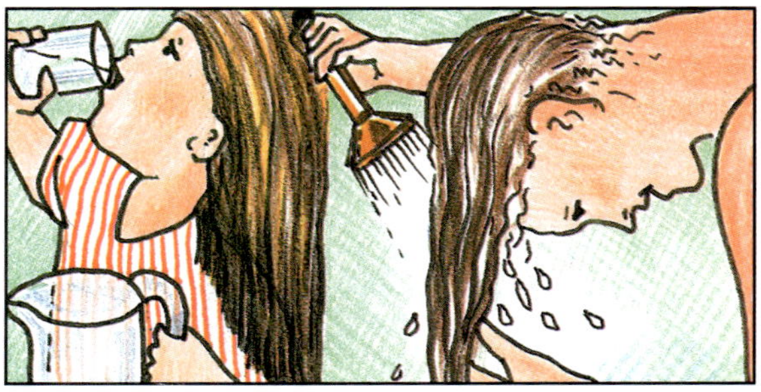

Eating Words

We eat food by chewing and swallowing. There are many different kinds of food which we eat to help us grow strong and healthy.

bathroom

razor

table

chair

shower

shelves

sink

lavatory

dining
room

bath

bunk beds

airport
lounge

ladder

window

bedroom

TV

armchair

chest of
drawers

sofa

double bed

lounge

Home Words

Home is the place where a person or family lives. Our home is comfortable. When children have grown up they may return to their family home for a holiday together with their parents.

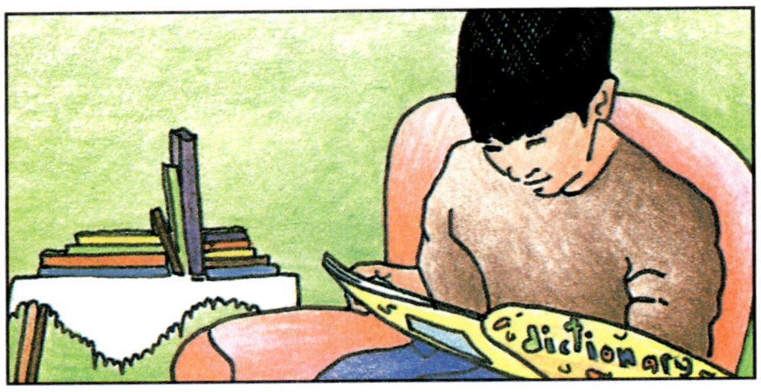

book

music

camera

photograph

comic

sewing

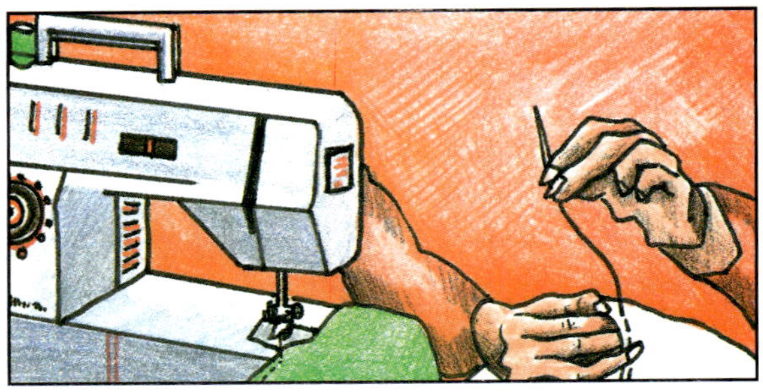

jigsaw

swimming

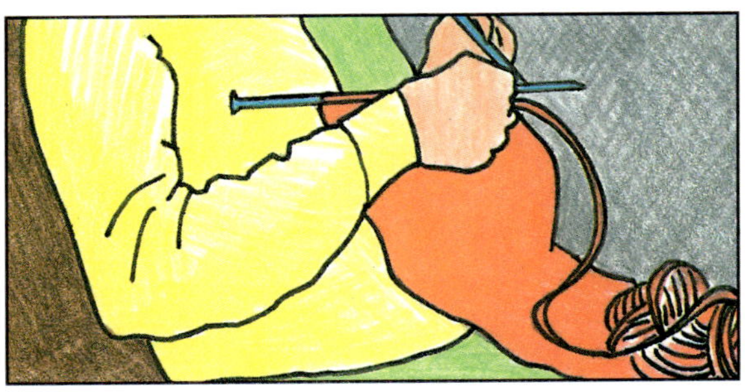

knitting

toys

mending

writing

Hobby Words

A hobby is something done regularly in your spare time for pleasure. Some people like to read books; some like to take photographs.

age

seven

arm

smile

elbow

aunt

neice

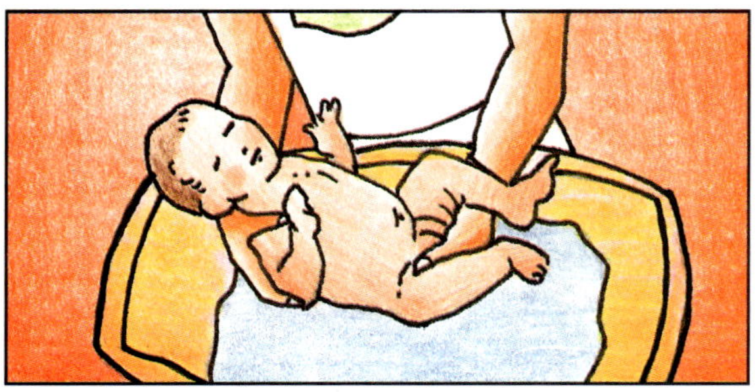

baby

bath

hand

blood

head

body

legs

feet

clothes

hat

jacket

jersey

leotard

People Words

mother daughter

woman father son boy girl children

family parents man baby

People are men, women and children. All of the men, women and children belonging to a tribe, race or nation are described as the people of that group.

My Word Book

Illustrated by Lesley McLaren

Copyright © 1993, LANDOLL
World Rights Reserved
LANDOLL
Ashland, Ohio 44805
No part of this book may be reproduced or copied in any form without written permission from the copyright owner. Printed in Canada. Manufactured in U.S.A.